—African-American Biographies—

MARY CHURCH TERRELL

Speaking Out for Civil Rights

Series Consultant:
Dr. Russell L. Adams, Chairman
Department of Afro-American Studies, Howard University

Cookie Lommel

Enslow Publishers, Inc.

40 Industrial Road	PO Box 38
Box 398	Aldershot
Berkeley Heights, NJ 07922	Hants GU12 6BP
USA	UK

http://www.enslow.com

Library of Congress Cataloging-in-Publication Data

Lommel, Cookie.
    Mary Church Terrell : speaking out for civil rights / Cookie Lommel.
      p. cm. — (African-American biographies)
    Summary: Traces the life and achievements of the black civil rights
worker whose greatest accomplishment, the integration of restaurants in
Washington, D.C., came when she was nearly ninety years old.
    Includes bibliographical references (p.) and index.
    ISBN 0-7660-2116-5 (hardcover)
    1. Terrell, Mary Church, 1863-1954—Juvenile literature. 2. African
American women—Biography—Juvenile literature. 3. African Americans—
Biography—Juvenile literature. 4. Civil rights workers—United States—
Biography—Juvenile literature. 5. African American women social
reformers—Biography—Juvenile literature. 6. African Americans—
Segregation—History—Juvenile literature. 7. African Americans—Civil
rights—History—Juvenile literature. [1. Terrell, Mary Church, 1863-1954.
2. Civil rights workers. 3. African Americans—Biography. 4. Women—
Biography.] I. Title. II. Series.
    E185.97.T47 L66 2003
    323'.092—dc21

                                 2002010401

Printed in the United States of America

10 9 8 7 6 5 4 3 2 1

To Our Readers:
We have done our best to make sure all Internet Addresses in this book were
active and appropriate when we went to press. However, the author and the
publisher have no control over and assume no liability for the material available
on those Internet sites or on other Web sites they may link to. Any comments or
suggestions can be sent by e-mail to comments@enslow.com or to the address on
the back cover.

Illustration Credits: Library of Congress, pp. 10, 14, 16, 25, 34, 50, 55,
58, 64, 73, 76, 78, 85, 90; Mary Church Terrell Papers/Moorland-
Spingarn Research Center, Howard University, pp. 8, 38, 45, 48, 71, 99,
101; Oberlin College Archives, p. 25; Special Collections, United States
Department of Defense, p. 95; University of Memphis Libraries, p. 10.

Cover Illustration: National Portrait Gallery, Smithsonian Institution

CONTENTS

Mary Church Terrell

1

LOST LAWS

On January 7, 1950, supported by a cane and a firm sense of right and wrong, Mary Church Terrell led a challenge to racial bigotry in Washington, D.C. The African-American crusader was nearly ninety years old, but age had not slowed her fight for equality and justice.

It was a quiet winter morning when Terrell and three friends, two black and one white, arrived at Thompson's Restaurant, two blocks from the White House. The laws of the time, known as "Jim Crow laws," allowed businesses to segregate (separate) black and white customers—even to refuse service to African Americans.

Under the Jim Crow laws, black people were kept apart from whites in everything from restaurants and hotels to rest rooms and drinking fountains. The laws called for services to be "separate but equal," but most facilities for African Americans were inferior and far from equal. Many people who tried to protest these laws were fined or thrown in jail.

Thompson's Restaurant was one of many in Washington, D.C., that would not serve African Americans. But on this cold winter day, Mary Church Terrell and her three friends, the Reverend William H. Jernagin, Geneva Brown, and David H. Scull, entered the whites-only cafeteria. David H. Scull, a white man, was a Quaker. His religion included strong moral beliefs that segregation was wrong.

In the cafeteria line, the four put bowls of soup on their trays. They had not even started to eat when they were asked to leave. The restaurant manager told Jernagin, "It is against the rules and regulations of the District to serve Negroes here."[1] Jernagin, a dignified minister who was president of the National Baptist Sunday School Convention, asked the manager, "Am I to understand that I am refused service because my face is black?"[2] The manager answered yes, just as Mary Church Terrell and her three friends had expected.

After peacefully leaving the restaurant, they put their plan for stopping racial discrimination in local restaurants into action. They turned to the law for help.

Before entering Thompson's Restaurant, Terrell and her companions had done their homework. What they learned about the nation's laws was very important. They believed that some almost eighty-year-old laws in Washington, D.C., supported their cause.

In 1872 and 1873, two anti-discrimination laws had been passed. The first law barred racial discrimination by hotels, barbershops, bathhouses, restaurants, and other public places in the nation's capital. In the second law, all Washington, D.C., eating places had been ordered by the courts to serve all respectable, well-behaved people. Restaurant owners who disobeyed this law would have to pay a $100 fine and risked losing their business licenses for a full year.

But even back in the 1880s the laws were unpopular and not often enforced. Business owners refused to change their behavior and obey the laws. African Americans who tried to be served at whites-only restaurants were still turned away. The laws were unpopular, and not often enforced. Business owners who broke the laws were not being punished.

After awhile the city courts tried to claim that the anti-discrimination laws were "repealed by implication" because they had not been followed for so long.[3]

Over time, something else happened. The two laws disappeared from many of the records kept for the public. By the early 1900s, they were no longer listed in the District Code of Laws.

Mary Church Terrell, fourth from the left, helped bring an end to segregation in Washington, D.C.

Mary Church Terrell's challenge to restaurant segregation was her first act as chairperson of the Coordinating Committee for the Enforcement of the District of Columbia Anti-Discrimination Laws. This committee had been formed when more than one hundred religious and civil rights organizations banded together to work for civil rights.

Terrell and the Coordinating Committee realized they could still use old legal codes to fight the Jim

Crow laws. If the old laws had never been officially repealed, then they would still be valid. That gave African Americans, and everybody else, the legal right to be served in any public place, so long as they were "respectable" and "well-behaved."

Few people were more respectable than Dr. Mary Church Terrell. She was well-educated, dignified, and certainly well-behaved. There were no valid reasons to refuse to serve her in a restaurant. So when Thompson's Restaurant refused to let Terrell and her friends eat their soup, she and the Coordinating Committee were ready to take legal action.

First, they brought a complaint about the restaurant to the District Corporation Counsel. They cited the laws of 1872 and 1873 to support their claim. The District Corporation Counsel agreed to weigh their complaint. For the next three years, the city and federal courts disagreed over whether the old laws, which came to be known as the "lost laws," were still valid.[4]

Eventually, the case was brought before the Supreme Court, the highest court in the United States. After forty days of arguments, the justices decided that the "lost laws" were still valid. On June 8, 1953, the Supreme Court declared that restaurants in Washington, D.C., could not discriminate on the basis of race. African Americans could not be turned away.

Terrell hailed the Supreme Court's decision, saying, "We will continue our efforts as long as

Mary Church Terrell dedicated her life to fighting racial injustice.

necessary to see that this law is accepted by all . . . and that no restaurant will be permitted to violate or evade it. We will not permit these laws to become lost again."[5]

Mary Church Terrell's battle to integrate the restaurants of Washington, D.C., was one of her most significant civil rights victories.

Mary Church Terrell made civil rights her life's work. All her life she used her gifts as a writer, public speaker, organizer, and leader to fight against injustice and racial discrimination. That added up to more civil rights accomplishments than will fit in one book. To present her many sides, the following pages focus on her varied accomplishments by chapter—from student to suffragette to writer. In the end, the total of her many accomplishments prove that she was indeed an American heroine.

2

A Child
of Privilege

When Mary Church was born, in 1863, it was common for African-American children to be discriminated against, even if their parents were rich. Mary's father, Robert Church, could afford to raise his family in the kind of financial comfort and ease more common among wealthy whites. But he, like Mary's mother, Louisa, was born a slave.

Mary's father was the son of his white master, Captain Charles B. Church, and Emmeline, the captain's African-American housemaid. Captain Church owned several riverboats that ran up and down the Mississippi River. After Robert's mother died,

Captain Church brought his son to work on his riverboats. Captain Church was very fond of his son and gave him everything that he could, except his freedom. Robert Church learned to do many different jobs well, and this helped him rise from the lowly position of dishwasher to procurement steward. Procurement steward was the highest job a slave was allowed to hold on a riverboat. As procurement steward, Mary's father bought food and goods in large quantities.

Robert Church worked hard to learn his father's riverboat business. He was twenty-four when the riverboat business was shut down during the Civil War. Then, after the Emancipation Proclamation of 1863 freed slaves in the South, he was free to build his own business. Robert chose to open a saloon, which became very successful. At about the same time he married Louisa Ayres.

Louisa Ayres was also one of the more fortunate slaves. She was a lady's maid in a household where her mother was the housekeeper. There, she was taught to read and write despite the fact that teaching slaves to read and write was against the law. She also learned to speak French.

Mary, Louisa and Robert's first child, was born in Memphis, Tennessee, on September 23, 1863, the same year that the Emancipation Proclamation was declared. Another child, Thomas, was born four years later.

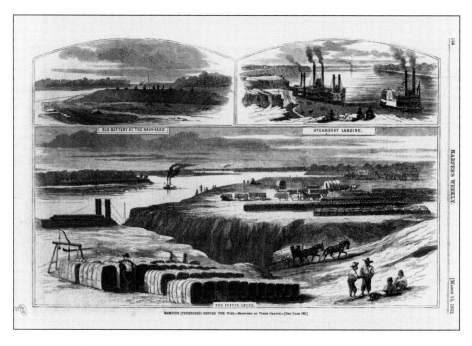

Both of Mary's parents were raised as slaves in the South, and freed after the Civil War. These pictures show Memphis, Tennessee, before the war.

Because of her father's business, Mary had a very good life for an African-American child. Memphis, at the time she was born, was filled with refugees from the Civil War. The quality of life for many in Memphis was very poor as the war dragged on. Mary was brought up in a world far apart from this.

Her father bought household supplies in bulk because of his experience in procuring items for his own father's ship. Because of this, Mary's home was filled with boxes of oranges and nuts, bunches of bananas, crates of chickens and turkeys, and big barrels of flour, lard, and butter. She and her brother never went hungry.

But her father's success at business did not make up for the color of his skin. Racism still affected him and gradually left its mark on his children. In 1866, when Mary was three years old, race riots broke out in Memphis. Black soldiers discharged from fighting in the Civil War clashed with the white police force of the city. Robert Church was one of the many victims of the fighting. He was shot in the back of the head in his saloon and left for dead. It was not a random shooting. Police and white business owners did not like to see successful African-American businesses competing with white ones.

Mary's father survived the bullet wound. A committee of congressmen came to Memphis to look into the details of the riot. They interviewed Mary's father. One of the congressmen was quite puzzled by Mary's father's looks. He asked, "How much of a colored man are you?" Mary's father replied, "I don't know . . . very little." [1] Mary's father had very light skin and had no trouble passing for white. Undaunted by the experience of the shooting, he went on to open another business.

Her mother was also a hard worker. Louisa Church was one of the first African-American women in the South to open and run her own hair salon. In the 1870s, bundles of false hair were used to create

Louisa Church ran a highly successful hair salon in Memphis.

elaborate hairstyles. Louisa Church excelled at this difficult task. Her salon, located off of Memphis' Court Square, attracted rich white socialites. When the Grand Duke Alexis of Russia came to Memphis, ladies who were going to the party in his honor came to Louisa Church's salon at seven o'clock in the morning to have their hair styled for the evening.

The success of the hair salon, along with the success of Robert's business, allowed the Church family the means to buy their first home as well as a carriage. Mary and her younger brother, Thomas, always had money for toys and clothing. They always had money for education. "My mother lavished money on my brother and me," Mary commented.[2] They were privileged children, and had many experiences ordinarily denied an African American in the nineteenth century. Mary's first friends were German children who lived in her suburban Memphis neighborhood. Often, Mary would return from her playmates' homes speaking German, confusing her mother.

Young Mary was called Mollie as a child, after one of her white grandfather's other children. Her world would have been safe and happy, were it not for one thing: the color of her skin.

Mary's parents tried to protect her from the past. They never talked about slavery. But Mary's grandmother, Eliza Ayres, did. Grandma Ayres was a marvelous storyteller. She told tales of Brother Rabbit and Brother Fox, and a hoop snake that chased after naughty children. "Run, chillun, run, the hoop snake's after you," she would say.[3] She also told stories about cruel masters and slave children who were sold away from their parents. Her stories often made Mary cry. "Never mind, honey," her grandma would comfort her.[4] "Grandma ain't a slave no more."[5]

Mary had a terrible experience when she was just four years old. A cat caught her mother's canary bird. She watched in horror as a woman who worked for her mother, along with some of her friends, beat the cat to death. Mary tried desperately to save the cat from this cruelty she could not understand.

Later, she realized that these women had been slaves. They had seen terrible beatings used to punish men, women, and children, and she believed this had shaped their later actions. Mary saw the killing of the cat as an example of slavery's damaging effects on future generations of African Americans.

Despite her parents' wealth, Mary faced her share of unhappiness as a child. Robert and Louisa Church divorced before Mary was five years old. Louisa Church was given custody of Mary and Thomas. They moved to a house near the hair salon. Robert Church wanted to take his son to live with him, and fought for custody in court. He lost. Divorce was uncommon at the time, and Mary was embarrassed by her parents' separate lives.

Even though he did not live with his children any more, Robert Church still spent time with Mary and Thomas. He made sure that his children went to the best schools available to African Americans at the time. He offered them generous support throughout their lives.

As Mary grew she had other unhappy experiences with racism. When she was five years old, she and her father traveled north by train. All African Americans had to sit in a separate coach reserved for "coloreds."[6] Some of the African Americans, including Robert Church, boldly sat in the white sections of the train. He then entered the smoker car, where Mary knew her father would mingle easily with white men. But Mary, sitting alone in the white section outside of the smoking coach, was harassed by the conductor collecting tickets, who called her a racist name and asked who she belonged to.

The conductor backed down after he discovered how rich Mary's father was, allowing her to stay in the best coach reserved for whites. But Mary was upset by the way the conductor had treated her. Worse, her father refused to explain to her what had happened, and told her never to talk of it again. But she kept trying. Mary later told her mother, and recalled that her mother seemed about to cry when Mary told her

Robert Church made his fortune as a businessman in post-Civil War Memphis.

that the conductor had called her a racist name. Mary explained to her mother that she had been a good girl. She had sat up straight and kept her dress clean and her hair tidy. She did not understand why the conductor had been so rude to her.

It hurt Louisa Church to explain to her much-loved daughter about racial discrimination. Mary would later say, "Seeing their colored children touched and seared and wounded by racial prejudice is one of the heaviest crosses which black women have to bear."[7]

3

EDUCATION WAS
HER LIFE

The greatest luxury that Robert Church ever gave his daughter was her education. And what an education! Any child of her era, no matter what the color of their skin, would have been lucky to attend the schools that Mary attended.

Robert Church was convinced that the Memphis schools could not offer the kind of education he wanted Mary to have. Most of the schools in Memphis had been destroyed in the race riots after the Civil War. The school that Mary had attended was in the basement of a church. Therefore, when Mary was only six years old, her parents decided to send her to

Antioch College Model School in Yellow Springs, Ohio. This was one of the most challenging schools in the country. Already Mary was a bright and spirited girl. During a school Christmas program, Mary had shown the audience an early taste of her fearlessness. She was the chosen "Queen" of the Christmas program, and she was required to wear a red dress and sit on a very high throne. But after a while she grew restless, and decided to jump from her high seat to the floor during the middle of the program. The audience was shocked, not just at the willfulness of her behavior, but because the throne was very high indeed.

Now in Yellow Springs she would need that spirited personality. Mary was the only African-American child in her class.

During her stay in Yellow Springs, Mary lived with the Hunsters. The Hunsters were an African-American family living near the school. They ran the town's only hotel and ice cream parlor. Although she was so young, Mary did not seem to mind moving away from her family. She already understood that she was in Ohio to better her education, and that was important to her. It helped that she was able to adapt easily to new situations, and the Hunsters were kind, loving people. They became Mary's second family and Yellow Springs became a second home. "I called Mrs. Hunster "Ma" and Mr. Hunster "Pa", Mary later said."[1]

Before she was old enough to travel back to Memphis by herself, Mary spent her summers in Yellow Springs with the Hunsters. She helped at the ice cream parlor. She explored. She read all the books she could get her hands on from the Sunday-school library. Ma Hunster taught her to recite poetry.

Whether at home in Memphis or in Yellow Springs, Mary was the spoiled daughter of a doting father. Stories were told about how much Robert Church indulged Mary. Once, Mary's father came to school to surprise her with a doll he had just bought. When he arrived, the teacher told him that Mary had been talking too much and could not keep still. In fact, the teacher admitted, Mary had just vanished from the classroom, only to be spotted crawling on the floor under the seats in order to reach the student sitting in front of her. The teacher did not think that Robert Church should reward Mary for this behavior by giving her the doll. He left it for her anyway.

Mary had an engaging personality and made friends easily. Even though she was the only black child in her grade, she was not often reminded of it. However, once, she was given the part of a stupid black servant in a school play. She refused the part realizing that it had been created to make her look foolish. Mary was, nonetheless, enthusiastic about her class assignments. She was always a top student throughout her years at Yellow Springs.

Mary chose the "gentlemen's" courses at Oberlin College to further challenge herself.

It was at school during a history lesson when Mary realized that she was the daughter of slaves. It had never occurred to her that her own mother and father had once been slaves. The connection to these oppressed people stunned and humiliated Mary.

During that dark history lesson, Mary made a promise to herself. She vowed that she would show her white teachers and classmates that she was not inferior to anyone, even if her ancestors had been slaves.

After four years at Yellow Springs, Mary's parents sent her to the public high school in Oberlin, Ohio, to begin the eighth grade. Mary's brother Thomas and her mother, meanwhile, moved from their home in Memphis, Tennessee, to New York City. In order to visit her parents during her summer vacations from school, Mary would take the train back and forth from Memphis to New York. Although Louisa Church would send Mary boxes of clothes and gifts during the school year, she rarely traveled to Ohio to visit her daughter.

Despite the distance between Mary and her family, she was happy at high school in Ohio. She found many opportunities for fun in addition to her studies. She was an official scorer for the all-male baseball games. She rode horses and learned to play tennis. She and her friends often spent time after supper practicing the latest dance steps, even though the school did not approve of dancing. Mary also found that she had a strong singing voice. She joined the Musical Union at the Oberlin Conservatory after the director urged her to use her vocal talents. Mary also used her vocal ability to recite poems to friends. Her favorite was:

> *Give me three grains of corn Mother,*
> *Give me three grains of corn,*
> *It will keep the little life I have,*
> *Till the coming of the morn.*"[2]

Mary grew up relying on her own considerable strength. At her high school graduation, she gave a speech titled "Troubles and Trials." She said that she felt most troubles were imaginary or could be worked through with a strong and cheerful attitude.[3]

During her teenage years, that cheerful attitude began to show itself in her choices and achievements.

After graduating from public high school in 1879, Mary enrolled at Oberlin College in Oberlin, Ohio. She kept trying to excel. At that time, many people believed that whites were more intelligent than blacks. As she entered college, Mary was determined to show her classmates otherwise.

Oberlin College itself was taking a stand in the fight against racism. The college was operated by abolitionists, people who had worked to eliminate slavery. Oberlin was one of the few colleges in America that was racially integrated (combined). Still, Mary was one of only a handful of African-American students at Oberlin. Few African Americans of her time were as rich as Mary's father. Most students did not have enough childhood education to enter Oberlin College.

Even in such a demanding college, Mary made a name for herself. Most women who enrolled in Oberlin chose the two-year "ladies'" course, but Mary decided to enter the four-year "gentlemen's" course of classical studies. She learned the languages of Latin and Greek. She also studied classical literature among other subjects. Mary did well in school and also made important friends. She became very popular among her classmates, and her professors thought highly of her. When Mary received high marks in Greek, her normally strict professor was quick to remark, "Miss Church, you should be proud of that record."[4] She participated in many campus and social activities. For example, she was one of only twelve students at Oberlin invited to join a newly formed lawn tennis club. Though blacks were usually assigned separate tables at mealtimes, Mary always had many invitations to sit with whites.

One day, Mary Church was approached by a young woman in the senior class and invited to join Aeolian, one of two literary clubs on campus. Mary knew the young woman was one of the most accomplished members of her class, and felt honored by this personal invitation. "I am happy I was invited to work in this club so early in the school year," Mary said.[5]

After joining Aeolian, Mary threw herself into the literary and parliamentary law required by the club. Years later these exercises would help her in her civil rights work. The club also stressed public debating skills, and Mary Church was elected in her sophomore and junior years to represent Aeolian during its annual competition with L.L.S., the other women's literary club at Oberlin.

She also improved her writing skills. Mary Church was one of the editors of her college newspaper, The Oberlin Review. In this newspaper, she saw the first article she had ever written appear in a printed publication. It was a proud moment for her.

But perhaps the proudest college moment of all was one of her first blows to racism and sexism. The English writer Matthew Arnold, a famous poet, was

Mary impressed her professors and fellow students at Oberlin College with her academic skills.

also an inspector of schools. His travels brought him to observe the Greek class in Oberlin College. Church was the only female student in a class of forty. Her teacher, Professor Frost, requested that she read from a Greek passage, and then translate it. Arnold believed that Africans and their descendants were unable to pronounce the Greek language. Mr. Arnold expressed great surprise with Mary's command of Greek. Church took great pleasure in proving him wrong.

Not every brush with racism ended in triumph. In her senior year, Church's great ability in creative writing caused her to be considered the class poet. But when it was time to elect the speaker for the Junior Exhibition, a young white man who had never displayed much talent in poetry won the position. Church and many of her classmates believed that his victory was caused by racism. Some of her classmates even scolded the young man for refusing to turn down the position, which they did not feel he had earned. "I know now, that blood can be thicker than water when many people elect one to represent them all," Mary said.[6]

Church's college years were remarkable in several ways. During this time, her father gained enormous riches. His success had brought him into contact with some of the black political leaders of the day. When Mary was seventeen, she received an invitation, along with her father, to go to Washington, D.C., to attend the inauguration of President James A. Garfield. She was able to meet some very important people during the week she was there. She met judges, congressmen and diplomats. But the person she was most interested in was Frederick Douglass. Douglass was born a slave in 1818, but escaped. He educated himself, and rose to fame as one of the world's greatest civil rights leaders. When Mary met him, he was the escort of the president-elect when he took the oath of office. After their meeting, Mary and Douglass remained friends for the rest of his life.

Mary's success during her college years was due, in large part, to her energy and intelligence. She had learned to ignore the small frustrations of being both black and a woman in a mostly white male program of studies. Church later said, "It would be difficult for a colored girl to go through a white school with fewer unpleasant experiences than I had."[7] When she graduated from Oberlin College in 1884 with a degree in the classics, she was one of the first African-American women to graduate from college in the United States. In her class commencement, three other black women received the B.A. (Bachelor of Arts) degree. Prior to that, only two black women had received that degree anywhere in the world.

In 1933, Church was named as one of the one hundred most successful students to graduate from Oberlin College. She could not have known then, that it was one of many awards she would win in her lifetime.

4

A Born Activist

hurch's next fight was for personal independence. The social rules governing women in the nineteenth century were very strong. Her father was adamant that she take her place as a socialite in Memphis when she graduated from Oberlin in 1884. Southern "ladies" did not work.[1] Professional women were socially outcast. Robert Church did not want his daughter to work for a living.

Instead, he invited her to live with him at his huge estate until the home he was building for her was complete. Her father had sent the blueprints, or floor plan, of Church's house to her while she was in college.

He celebrated her arrival in Memphis with a fantastic dinner party. Now that her college education was complete, Mary was expected to take over the running of her father's household. She also was expected to entertain guests. But Mary was keenly aware of the opportunities she had as an educated woman and was not interested in these activities. She had prepared herself to work. She spent a restless winter in Memphis wondering how to tell her father how she felt.

The following January, Robert Church remarried. He married a schoolteacher named Anna Wright, an accomplished piano player. Mary Church knew and liked Wright, a friend of her mother's. As a matter of fact, Wright had taught Mary Church to play the piano. Church approved of her father's marriage.

After the wedding, Mary Church thought seriously about how to leave Memphis. With Wright in the household, Mary felt she was less necessary in the social obligations Robert insisted upon. She believed that her college education was going to waste, and she was not satisfied with the rounds of parties and social activities that had occupied her time. Church decided that it was time to discover her purpose in life. She felt strongly that it was her duty to get out and work toward ending racism.

She made up her mind to become a teacher even though Robert Church was firm in his belief that privileged ladies were not supposed to work.

Mary was strongly influenced by her first meeting with Frederick Douglass.

Housework and hostessing had been the way of life in the South for three centuries, and he wanted his daughter to follow tradition.

Finally, Church decided to defy him. She chose to leave Memphis, despite her father's wishes, and to continue the independent journey she had begun in college. She secretly sent out letters to schools asking about teaching positions. While waiting for responses, she spent the summer in New York with her mother. Several schools for African Americans responded to her inquiries, and offered attractive teaching positions.

In 1885, she accepted a teaching position at Wilberforce College in Ohio. Upon her arrival, Church taught five classes in a variety of subjects, including French, mineralogy, reading, and writing. She also served as secretary of the faculty, where she was required to take notes in longhand no matter how busy her schedule was. "No one could truthfully claim that I had many idle moments."[2] In addition, she was the church organist for services every Sunday morning and evening, and spent one night every week at choir rehearsal. Her salary was $40 per month, out of which she had to pay for her food. Her room was given to her free of charge.

Meanwhile, in Memphis, her father had found out about his daughter's job teaching at Wilberforce. He refused to speak to her. His silence lasted almost a year. During her first year at Wilberforce, she received only one letter from her father.

At the conclusion of her first year teaching at Wilberforce, Church visited her mother in New York. While there, she decided it was time to reconcile with her father in Memphis. En route to Tennessee, she sent a wire to her father, informing him of her arrival time. She breathed a sigh of relief when he met her train at the station. After a year of little communication, Robert Church had finally decided to support his daughter in her career choice. He never again tried to prevent her from fulfilling her goals.

After that summer vacation, Church spent her second year teaching at Wilberforce, this time with her father's approval. At the close of her second year, a very rich woman visited the school, became fond of Church's work, and invited her to travel to Europe during summer vacation. Church agreed to this trip only after seeking her father's approval. He gave his enthusiastic permission, and promised to give her as much money as she needed. "I was the happiest girl on earth. The world is mine, I am going to Paris."[3]

But at the same time, Church received an important job opportunity. She was invited to teach in Washington D.C., at Washington's Colored High School (officially known as the M Street High School). It was the leading public high school in the country for black students. The invitation came from Dr. John R.

Francis, one of the few African-American members of the Board of Education. He had reached out to the secretaries of several colleges, requesting the records of recent African-American graduates, so that he might offer them positions in Washington's Colored High School.

Church suddenly found herself in a dilemma. She had eagerly looked forward to the European trip with her rich friend, but she did not want to pass up the opportunity to teach in the nation's capital.

Her father tried to help her decide. He offered to travel abroad with her himself if she waited until the following summer. Assured of a travel companion, Church finally decided to accept the job in Washington.

While teaching in the District of Columbia in 1888, Terrell completed the master of arts degree from Oberlin. She was now one of the few well-educated African-American women in the nation.

She worked in the Colored High School's Latin department under the direction of Robert Heberton Terrell, a light-skinned mulatto (of mixed race) born in Orange, Virginia, in 1857. Terrell had graduated with honors from Harvard College in 1884. Mary Church and Robert Terrell had more than a few things in common. They were very attracted to one another, though Church did not want a serious commitment at the time.

Robert Church wanted Mary to return home after college to be a Southern "lady."

Her father continued to remind her of their planned "Grand Tour" of Europe. The Grand Tour was a popular activity for rich young men and women in the nineteenth century. It was a trip designed to learn the cultural ways of Europeans. Robert Church allowed his daughter to decide their destinations. She included stops in England, Belgium, Italy, Germany, Switzerland, and France. Mary and Robert Church stayed in France for three months, before Robert Church had to return to his work in Memphis. Mary Church continued to study in France for a year before moving on to Germany. "My father assured me that he had perfect confidence in me no matter where I traveled. "I know you can take care of yourself," he wrote."[4] She arrived in the German capital of Berlin, and immediately adjusted to the language she had learned as a child from her friends in Memphis. Her early exposure to German allowed her to feel comfortable in Germany quickly. Mary loved to attend the German Opera, "I was having the time of my life."[5]

While in Germany, she received frequent visits from her mother, father, and brother, Thomas. During her first winter in the city, Louisa Church wrote that she and Thomas would dock in Liverpool, England, since she had won the Louisiana State Lottery! Louisa Church wasted no time in spending her winnings. She stayed at the most expensive hotels, and even traveled to France for the Paris Exposition of 1889. After a satisfying trip, Church's mother and brother sailed from Hamburg, Germany, back to the United States.

Mary Church moved on to Florence, Italy, the center of artistic culture in Europe. There, she spent countless hours in art galleries studying the works of the world's greatest painters. She studied the works of art until she was able to determine the artist simply by looking at the characteristics of a painting.

In Florence, Church received a telegram announcing her father's arrival.[6] He brought with him his new family. He and his wife, Anna, now had two young children, Robert and Annette.

Mary Church spent the following year traveling through Europe. She attended plays, concerts, and exhibitions, perfecting her foreign-language skills. She wrote her diaries in French and in German. In those languages, she expressed her joy at finally being free of America's racial tension. She had found Europeans to be very friendly toward her and curious about her ancestry. She had been able to enjoy people without thinking about their race. Church often thought of staying in Europe to escape the race problem in America. Once she was stopped by a woman who said, "I have heard you are American, but you are too dark to be American aren't you?" Mary laughingly replied, "I am a dark American."[7]

During her trip, several white European men had asked her to marry them. Church refused all of their offers, feeling that marrying a non-black would cause her to lose touch with her African-American roots. Deep down, Church felt the need to return to her own beloved country and to fight the racism that was so damaging to African-American children. She knew that she could not accomplish this by remaining in Europe. She would find a way to use her education and energy for the betterment of her people. In 1890, she decided to board a steamer bound for New York City. She was coming home.

5

THE TURNING POINT

Shortly after her return from Europe, Church received a letter from Robert Heberton Terrell. In the letter, Terrell strongly requested her immediate return to Washington, D.C. He wanted her to resume her teaching position at Washington's Colored High School.

Church left her mother's home in New York City and returned to Washington, D.C. She was immediately re-appointed to her position, and spent the following school year teaching mostly Latin and German.

While Church traveled Europe, Robert Terrell had been making his own accomplishments. He had taught at the M Street School in Washington, D.C., from 1884 to 1889. At the same time, he was a practicing lawyer in a law firm he opened with John Roy Lynch, an African-American man who had served in the United States House of Representatives during the more liberal years of the Reconstruction period. In 1889, Terrell was appointed Chief of Division, Office of the Fourth Auditor of the Treasury Department. Church was very pleased by Robert Terrell's accomplishments and connections. He liked her, and they began to date. Terrell finally proposed to Church in October of 1891. They were to be married the following year.

But several months before summer vacation began in 1892, Church received a letter from A.A.F. Johnston, the dean of women at Oberlin College. The letter invited her to take over the position of school registrar. (A registrar is the person responsible for registering students and maintaining their records.) Church was aware that the position had always been filled by a white person, and that her acceptance of the invitation would be a positive step for African Americans.

Church considered postponing the October wedding in order to accept the position as registrar. Again, she found herself making a choice between her personal desires and her professional goals. This time, after carefully weighing both sides, Church decided to put her personal life first. She remembered, "I decided to write to Oberlin declining the position. I was unhappy indeed."[1] She decided to go ahead with her plans to marry Terrell in October.

During the summer before her marriage, Church stayed in New York with her mother to prepare for the wedding. Mary Church and Robert Terrell finally became husband and wife in October of 1892. Mary Church Terrell's father celebrated the union with a huge feast of turkey, roast pig, salads, ice cream, and wine. The Memphis Commercial Appeal newspaper wrote of the event, "As they discussed the elaborate menu and drank the excellent champagne of the host, the guests were regaled with the sensuous strains of Joe Hall's orchestra, which, hidden in an alcove, made the air sweet with its beautiful music."[2]

After the wedding, the couple visited Louisa Church, Mary Church Terrell's mother, in New York, before spending some time in Boston, Massachusetts. Soon after, they returned to Washington, where Robert Terrell resumed his duties as a division chief in the Office of the Treasury.

Because, at that time, married women were legally barred from working as teachers, Mary Church Terrell decided to focus all of her energy on managing her household, something she had never had to do. She had been sent away to school at age six, and was hastily run out of the kitchen any time she had attempted to cook during her summer vacations. Although married women were responsible for all of the household

Mary married Robert Terrell in 1892. He would become the first African-American judge in Washington, D.C.

entertaining and housekeeping, college-bred women like Mary Church Terrell were not knowledgeable about such things. Typically, she resolved to prove that college women were not only able to manage household chores, but could do them as well as anyone else.

Her first experience in housekeeping brought her enjoyment. She looked upon her tasks as daily challenges. Soon, she found herself applying fresh coats of ivory paint to four rooms of the house. She also canned and preserved large quantities of fruit every fall, a ritual she would perform for many years to come. She taught herself to sew and reupholstered the parlor sofa.

Preparing the first Thanksgiving meal was her first domestic test, however. It was a disaster. After watching a big football game in town, Robert Terrell returned home expecting that a full dinner had been prepared. However, what he saw was an empty table and a wife attempting to act as if nothing was wrong.

Mary Church Terrell struggled with that Thanksgiving dinner for several more hours, until 10:00 p.m., when the food was finally ready. From that day forward, her husband teased her about her cooking skills, and would often joke about the time that her Thanksgiving dinner took twelve hours to cook.[3]

She also faced her share of real sorrows. During the early years of her marriage, she became pregnant three times in five years. All three of her pregnancies ended in miscarriages. She attributed the miscarriages to the poor medical facilities available to African-American women at that time. The loss of her children sent her into a deep depression, which lasted for months.

During her fourth pregnancy, the doctor advised her to get away from everything that reminded her of the pain. At her husband's insistence, she left for New York to be with her mother. Her mother's cheerful disposition helped her recover from her losses. There, in her mother's home, Terrell finally gave birth to a healthy baby girl in 1898. The baby was named Phyllis, after the black poet Phyllis Wheatley.

But as she was building her family, a horrific event was taking place that changed her career path forever. It brought her back into a passionate fight against racism. In 1892 her old and dear friend Tom Moss was lynched by an angry white mob that was jealous of his financial success.

Terrell and Moss were childhood friends in Memphis, Tennessee. For many years he was a mailman, but he saved his money until he had enough to open his own store. His store was located in the Memphis suburbs, and he had several other black men as his partners in the enterprise. Soon, the black citizens in the area began going to Moss's store, and stopped trading at the white business across the street. Moss's goods were less expensive, and Moss was known

Mary Church Terrell brought her daughter Phyllis with her on many of her lectures and public appearances.

for treating his African-American customers with respect. The white owner of the other store did not.

The white storekeeper decided to vandalize Moss's store in retaliation for losing his customers. The local police, who were also racist, arrested Moss. The next night they hung him. It could have been just another lynching (there were 225 in 1892 alone) but this one was different. It caught the attention of Mary Church Terrell. And she was not alone in her outrage. Ida B. Wells-Barnett was a newspaper editor and friend of Moss's. She would fight back against lynching through her writing.

Terrell had read of countless such lynchings. "I had been deeply disturbed by these acts."[4] But this one, the death of her friend, jarred her faith in the Christian religion. She could not understand how any God could allow such a terrible thing to happen.

Her sadness eventually turned to action. She began to speak out against racism. Terrell, along with prominent abolitionist Frederick Douglass, made an appointment with the President of the United States, Benjamin Harrison, to ask for his help in the fight. They were disappointed. Although Harrison listened to them, he took no steps to prevent further injustices.

But Terrell did not give up. She continued to speak out. During the late nineteenth century, many African-American women's service clubs were established in order to address important social issues. Typically,

SOUTHERN HORRORS.

LYNCH LAW

IN ALL

ITS PHASES

Miss IDA B. WELLS,

Price, · · · Fifteen Cents.

THE NEW YORK AGE PRINT,

1892.

Ida B. Wells joined Terrell in her fight against racial injustice by writing about lynchings in newspapers.

these clubs were refused admittance to larger national clubs, like the National Council of Women and the General Federation of Women's Clubs. But Terrell would not allow discrimination to keep her from speaking out.

Realizing that membership in a national club offered the opportunity to address issues like racism, Terrell became the leader of a new club formed in Washington, D.C. It was called the Colored Woman's League. It was to have a powerful effect on history. "I knew what could be accomplished as a group, so I joined enthusiastically."[5] Three years later, African-American women in Boston, under the leadership of Josephine St. Pierre Ruffin, formed the Federation of African-American Women. Margaret Murray Washington, the wife of activist and scholar Booker T. Washington, was elected president of the Boston organization.

In 1896 the two groups, along with other African-American women's organizations, merged to become the powerful National Association of Colored Women. Terrell was elected to be their first president. "There was every reason for all who have the interest of the race at heart, to associate with this League," Terrell announced.[6] This leadership position was the first important step in her long journey for women's civil rights and for an end to racial segregation.

6

THE LECTURE CIRCUIT

s President of the National Association of Colored Women, (NACW), Terrell took on issues that ranged from lynching and Jim Crow laws to the rights of women.

Under Terrell's leadership, the NACW established many children's training and parenting programs. The organization wanted to improve living and working conditions in black communities. One of their most important projects was the creation of kindergartens and day nurseries for working African-American mothers. The organization also founded evening schools for adults, settlement houses for migrant women, orphanages, clinics, and homes for the aged.

The group helped in the fight against racism and sexism, actively supporting voting rights for all women. At that time, women did not have the right to vote. As the NACW President, Terrell spoke out frequently regarding the group's ideas, or platforms. One way to achieve these goals was through educating the public. Much of her work included meeting with, and speaking to, white women's groups devoted to getting women the vote (called "suffrage").[1] Also deeply concerned about education, Terrell sold her speeches to raise money for a kindergarten.

Terrell felt hopeful that the world could change if enough good people were motivated. In 1898 she delivered a speech before the National American Women's Suffrage Association. It was called "The Progress of Colored Women." Terrell always believed in her dream. She began her speech:

"Fifty years ago a meeting such as this, planned, conducted, and addressed by women would have been an impossibility. Less than forty years ago, few sane men would have predicted that either a slave or one of his descendants would, in this century at least, address such an audience in the Nation's Capital at the invitation of women representing the highest, broadest, best type of womanhood that can be found anywhere in the world."[3]

The Colored American newspaper called her speech a "revelation."[4] The newspaper also wrote, "She spoke for a half hour with power and fascination of manner such as few women possess." This optimistic speech was the first of many Terrell would give on the lecture circuit, on behalf of the NACW and of the women's rights movement. For example, in 1900, Terrell gave a thirty-minute presentation before the same group. The topic was "Justice of Women's Suffrage."[5]

Terrell's reputation as a remarkable speaker grew. She crafted each speech very carefully in order to make the subject of racism understandable to the average person. She gave her lectures catchy names like "The Bright Side of a Dark Subject."[6] She enjoyed public speaking and felt that every time she spoke to an audience of white people, she put black women in a more positive light.

Even though Terrell loved the lecture circuit, she often had to leave her family for three weeks at a time. She wrote to her husband, "This is a strenuous life I'm leading. I have to get up and take five or six o'clock trains in the morning, when I reach the place at which I pass the night about eleven or twelve . . . It is a great sacrifice for me to leave home, I tell you." But her sense of duty kept her going.[7]

Robert Terrell was always supportive of his wife's career. Even when friends warned him about how her work might spoil their marriage, he continued to

Mary Church Terrell worked tirelessly to earn all women, white and black, the right to vote.

encourage her to accept every opportunity to speak on her views. He, along with the help of Mary Church Terrell's mother, would keep the household running smoothly and the children well cared for.

In 1904, Mary Church Terrell spoke at the International Congress of Women in the city of Berlin, Germany. She was the only person of color invited to attend. She was determined to make a good impression as the only representative of African Americans present. She drew on her education and on her previous experience to do so.

She noticed that the German-speaking women were growing restless with the English speakers, who did not speak in the language of their hosts. Terrell delivered her own speech in German. Then she recited the speech in French as well as in English. She created much excitement with her abilities. After the address, which had been "Progress of Colored Women," she was flooded with invitations to speak throughout the world.

For almost thirty years, Terrell continued to work with both black and white suffrage organizations. She was invited by the Slayton Lyceum Bureau to become a professional lecturer. She traveled the world, speaking of progress since Emancipation, racial injustices that still existed, lynching, the woman's right to vote, economics, crime, and African-American history and culture.

In 1937, she represented black women at the World Fellowship of Faiths held in London, England. Terrell had the opportunity to meet many of the most famous leaders of the women's movement, including Susan B. Anthony, Jane Addams, and Carrie Chapman Catt.

Terrell was a great speaker. She chose to memorize all of her speeches so that she would not have to look at notes. The creative writing style she used in her speeches encouraged her interest in publishing articles on social issues. In fact, Terrell's real ambition was to be a writer. She worked on her articles with as much enthusiasm as she did with her speeches. She tried to present them in a popular, readable style. Many newspapers and journals worldwide carried her work.

7

WOMEN'S RIGHTS

During her years of lecturing, Terrell came to aid the cause for women's rights along with the African-American cause. The issue of race complicated and divided the women's rights movement. Race was a strong issue for women even after the passage of the Nineteenth Amendment to the Constitution, which granted women the right to vote.

In the fight for voting rights, many white southerners opposed rights for black women. Northern white suffragists feared the loss of the southerners' support. They did not easily welcome

Susan B. Anthony was one of the pioneers of the women's suffrage movement, and a good friend to Mary Church Terrell.

black women into their national organization before 1920. Mary Church Terrell tried to break that pattern.

By attending a meeting of the National American Woman Suffrage Association, Terrell was able to meet Susan B. Anthony. Susan B. Anthony was one of the pioneers of the women's rights movement. "Are you a member of this Association?" Anthony asked Terrell.[1] "No I am not," Mary replied, "but I thought you might be willing to listen to an appeal for justice by an outsider."[2] Anthony was impressed with Terrell's work and invited her to write a resolution that would be added to those the suffrage association upheld. This invitation began a long and wonderful friendship between the two women, lasting until Anthony's death. As a symbol that signaled the beginning of that friendship, Anthony sent her a brochure entitled, History of Woman Suffrage. On that brochure she wrote: "Mrs. Mary Church Terrell, from her sincere friend and co-worker, Susan B. Anthony, Rochester New York, February 15, 1898."[3]

In the beginning, the National American Woman Suffrage Association met in Washington every two years. When Terrell attended, she witnessed an impressive gathering. Women from all over the world were there, all interested in women's rights. The women running the meeting were the leaders of this cause, Elizabeth Cady Stanton, Lucretia Mott and Susan B. Anthony. At the end of the meeting, one of the leaders asked all the women who believed in suffrage for women to stand up. Terrell recalled that though the auditorium was filled that day, few women stood.[4] Though it was difficult for her, she forced herself to rise to her feet. In the early 1890s, it required a lot of courage to stand up in public for the rights of women. It was not a popular cause.

Several years after she gave her first speech to the National American Woman Suffrage Association, the group invited Terrell to address them for a second time. The committee asked Terrell to speak as a woman, without regard to race. The subject was "The Justice of Woman Suffrage." She would be the keynote speaker for that evening.[5] Realizing the importance of every word, Terrell poured her soul into everything she said. The audience gave her a standing ovation. In the February 10, 1900 issue of *The Boston Transcript*, an article carried the headline, "Mrs. Mary C. Terrell's Address Able and Brilliant."[6] The article read:

> The Friday evening session of the suffrage convention brought before a very large audience, a woman of whom few present had heard, but whose address was one of the ablest and most brilliant to which a Washington audience may listen. The woman was Mrs. Mary Church Terrell, a member of the School Board of the District of Columbia, a graduate of Oberlin College and president of the National Association of Colored Women. Her topic was "The Justice of Woman Suffrage," and she combated the old objections with earnest argument, biting

sarcasm and delightful raillery. At her close the applause lasted several minutes.

Highlighting the importance of that speech, *The Boston Transcript* again reviewed her work in an editorial on February 19, 1900. The writer of the article quoted large segments of her speech.[7] He heaped praise upon every word. Terrell's friendship with Susan B. Anthony continued to blossom. She was asked to give a speech to the Political Equality Club, where Anthony was a member. Anthony gave a reception for Terrell in her home and introduced her to many of her personal friends. Terrell remembered how she had read about Anthony when she was a student in college. She had secretly supported Anthony's cause. Little did she realize that fate would have her as a guest in her home.

Terrell and Anthony had much in common. Anthony was born into a Quaker family on a farm near Adams, Massachusetts. Before Anthony was sixteen years old, she began teaching. In 1848, Anthony attended the first Woman's Rights Convention held in Seneca Falls, New York, with her sister Mary. During the 1850s she became increasingly interested in women's rights. She met Elizabeth Cady Stanton in Seneca Falls, and they became lifelong friends. By 1854, Anthony was organizing petition drives. She went door to door getting signatures to present to lawmakers.

Though she never lost interest in her commitment to women's rights, the approaching Civil War drew her attention to the anti-slavery movement. She poured a great deal of energy into working for the people who wanted to end slavery. Just as Terrell would soon be committed to civil rights, Anthony became an anti-slavery advocate. She was constantly speaking in public, often to violent and hostile crowds. Anthony, with her friend Elizabeth Cady Stanton, organized petition drives to free slaves. They secured hundreds of thousands of signatures to help win the freedom of African-Americans. After the Civil War, Anthony again focused on women's rights, until her death in 1906.

Another of Terrell's friends, Frederick Douglass, had been actively involved in the women's rights movement. Douglass was significant to the cause because of his unique involvement in its early development. In an 1848 meeting, when Elizabeth Cady Stanton first presented a resolution demanding equal political rights for women, many in the group were so shocked that they tried to stop her. Even the bravest of women at the meeting did not want to tackle this difficult, though worthy, issue. Douglass however, stood up in support of her resolution.

It was mainly due to his masterful arguments and powerful presentation that this resolution passed. Douglass put an unforgettable stamp on the women's movement. After Douglass's death in 1895, Terrell was honored by an invitation to represent him at the sixtieth anniversary of the Women's Rights Convention in Seneca Falls, New York.

As women's suffrage became a mass movement in America, a similar movement was being carried out in Britain. In 1914, Alice Paul and other American women, who had been training British women, returned to the U.S. Here, they formed a more militant organization that went on hunger strikes and frequently picketed the White House. Terrell joined Paul in picketing The White House.

Shortly after the onset of the first World War (1914-1918), Terrell and her daughter Phyllis joined Alice Paul and Lucy Burns of the Congressional Union for Women's Suffrage (CUWS). Terrell and Phyllis joined the picket line outside of the White House. Terrell was concerned about the lack of support for black women's suffrage. This was a thorny issue among white women in the movement, who believed that including black women in the fight for voting rights would involve the race problem. It was feared that the alliance with black civil rights leaders would lose the support of white women in the South.

Terrell experienced this indignity firsthand when she was demonstrating in front of the White House. Leaders of the suffrage movement asked the African-American Ida B. Wells-Barnett not to march with other, white members. Even after pressure from

Suffragist Alice Paul, shown here at a protest, was reluctant to support the black woman's right to vote movement.

people like Terrell White Ovington, a white supporter of women's rights who was involved in black civil rights after hearing Frederick Douglass speak in a Brooklyn church, the CUWS refused to support the rights of black women to vote.[8]

Though both women were on the side of women's rights, an uneasy relationship existed between Alice Paul and Terrell. Paul headed the National Woman's Party and publicly affirmed the right for all women to vote. Yet her actions often countered this view. She urged women to change the laws nationally, not certain states. Many historians believe that it was Paul's leadership that led to a successful passage of the suffrage amendment in 1919.

On August 18, 1920, the Nineteenth Amendment gave women the right to vote in America. It was ratified (confirmed and signed) by President Woodrow Wilson. Terrell's writing, lecturing, and protests, like that of other suffragettes, paid off.

Unfortunately, this achievement was not reached without the sacrifice of African-American women's rights. Most southern white women did not support black suffrage. They decided to support "educated suffrage," which excluded many African-American men and women. Northern white women realized that they needed the power of white southern women to get the suffrage amendment passed. Paul was very concerned about offending southern white women supporters.

Paul would never publicly state that she endorsed black women's suffrage.

Walter White, head of the NAACP at the time, wrote a letter to Mary Church Terrell regarding Alice Paul. He referred to statements made by Alice Paul in a speech she gave in South Carolina, " . . . that all this talk of Negro women voting in South Carolina was nonsense."[9] Paul clearly was behind white women's suffrage alone.

After 1920 and the passing of the suffrage amendment, southern black women who tried to vote were excluded from doing so for various reasons. They were asked to have certain educational and character requirements, or they were asked to pay poll taxes. Alice Paul and the National Woman's Party did nothing to stop this. She argued that these were racial issues, not women's issues. When Mary Church Terrell asked Alice Paul whether she supported the enforcement of the nineteenth amendment for all women, Paul refused to say that she did.[10]

8

SERVING EDUCATION

While lecturing, Terrell continued her work in education. In 1895, she was appointed to the District of Columbia school board. She was one of the first African-American women to serve in the position. Congress had given the commissioners of the district permission to appoint three women to the board. About one-third of the population of the district was black at that time.

Dr. C. B. Purvis, the son of a famous Philadelphia abolitionist, suggested that Terrell be appointed to the school board. Her qualifications and education were remarkable. Terrell was honored by the request, but she was pregnant with another child, whom she later miscarried, and could not take the job. But Terrell chose her replacement. She did not believe that the commissioners were qualified to do so.

She told Commissioner Ross, head of the District's educational affairs: "Without intending to do so, white people who have the power of placing colored people in responsible positions often appoint individuals who misrepresent their race instead of representing it well, because they are not well enough acquainted with colored people to know whom to select. Please don't make this mistake in this case."[1]

Commissioner Ross listened to her plea, and then asked Terrell about herself. The commissioner asked where she had been educated, "Have you any letters from your former teachers at Oberlin?"[2] He was impressed by her education and travels, and even asked her opinion on several issues related to public schools. Later that night, a reporter rang her doorbell. He wanted a quote from one of the first African-American women on the Board of Education![3]

Terrell changed her mind and accepted the job. It was her goal to use the job to work for the equal treatment of African-American students and faculty in Washington's segregated school system.

Terrell's smooth integration of the board comforted those who believed she would be snubbed by the white female board members. No one, she believed, discounted her opinion on the board because she was black.

Once she settled into her new position, she focused her attention on changing the fact that there were no Easter holidays for the District of Columbia's students. Other teachers, black and white, helped her collect information from other school systems that suggested both teachers and students did better with a break from school activity. Terrell presented her findings to the board, and the trustees granted a short Easter break. This was the first of her many successes on the school board.

Another was the passing of the Douglass Day holiday. Terrell felt that the life of Frederick Douglass should be used as an example to schoolchildren. Douglass' many achievements proved how far a black person is able to reach in America. She argued that Douglass Day should be celebrated.

The board agreed. Valentine's Day, the fourteenth of February, became Douglass Day. On the fourteenth, songs of freedom were sung. Douglass' famous essays were read. Douglass Day was the first school holiday in any city that celebrated an African-American leader. The New York Age commented, "Mrs. Mary Church Terrell conceived the idea of celebrating the life of Frederick Douglass, and it was immediately adopted."[4]

Terrell also managed to arrange a salary for a director of music for black schools. During a time when music was considered unnecessary, this was another bonus for the children. She struggled continuously to see that all children, black and white, received a good education.

Terrell was also concerned with the way in which a student was admitted into normal school. ("Normal school" was a school where teachers were trained.) Students until then had to take a test and face a medical exam upon graduation from high school. The admission tests had many critics. Angry parents of students who failed, complained that the oral portion of the test was unfair. It counted for twenty-five percent of the final grade. Students who were less skilled in expressing themselves in the spoken word were more likely to fail. "This caused much bitterness," Terrell said.[5] She felt that all high school graduates should automatically be entered in normal school. The board passed this resolution as well.

Her school board activities often took her to the halls of the United States Congress. She tried to get Congress to give money to public schools for buildings, salaries, and other needs. She also made the rounds of the schools in her district in order to form closer ties with the teachers. She felt that it was good to get to know each teacher personally, and to learn their attitudes toward their students. She believed this extra knowledge would help her with both the teachers and the students.

Board of Education member Mary Church Terrell fought for a higher quality of education for Washington, D.C., school children.

Terrell headed to the United States Congress another time. Congress was in charge of the money given to her school district. She argued that a black administrator should receive the same pay as a white administrator. Her arguments were not strong enough in their opinion. One congressman commented, "Four thousand dollars! (the amount a white administrator received). Why, no colored man is worth that much."[6]

Major racial problems did not affect her time on the school board, but equality was still not achieved. The school board, for example, rarely voted on matters relating to African-American schoolchildren unless all three African-American board members were united on the issue. Remarkably, Terrell managed to get two men appointed to important teaching positions without the approval of the other two African-American board members. She wanted the rest of the board to vote based on a man's qualifications, not on the color of his skin or her own skin. "As I look back on my record with the Board, I am happy I did everything I could to promote the welfare of the students," Terrell commented.[7]

In 1901, after serving on the board for nearly six years, Terrell resigned when her husband became the principal of the M Street School for colored children. She knew that it would be a conflict of interest for her to work for the school board while he was the principal. She received many letters from people who

Terrell often argued for equality between black and white schools in Washington, D.C.

were unhappy that she was leaving, and many thanks for what she had already done.

Later, the United States Congress decided to redesign the Board of Education. They decided that judges should now choose the board members. The judges decided that no one who had been on the old school board, except Terrell, should serve again. She served for the second time from 1906 to 1911.

After her second term on the school board, the people of Washington honored her by giving her a testimonial dinner. Dozens of important people came to speak and to give her flowers and a statue of Venus de Milo.[8] All those she had helped appreciated Terrell's devotion to education.

9

THE NAACP CALLS

errell used her education to help African Americans and other people of color fight for equality. In her lifetime, the problem of racism rose again and again, and the African-American community was deeply divided over the solutions. At the heart of the controversy were Terrell's friends and peers, Booker T. Washington and W.E.B. Du Bois.

Du Bois was one of the great thinkers of the twentieth century and one of the early members of the NAACP (National Association for the Advancement of Colored People). He was also an outspoken opponent of Booker T. Washington, another famous

W. E. B. Du Bois called on African Americans to fight for their rights.

African American. Du Bois and Washington seriously disagreed on the best way for African Americans to advance.

Washington was often called an "accommodationist," which meant that he felt that people of color should work with the system that already existed instead of trying to change it.[1] He felt that blacks shouldn't spend their energy and money trying to achieve equal civil and political rights that whites took for granted. He felt that it was best for African Americans to concentrate instead on improving their economic skills and the quality of their character.

What this meant was that the burden of improving their status should rest solely on the shoulders of the African Americans.

Washington thought that eventually, the black man who pursued accommodation by improving himself would earn the love and respect of the white man, and civil and political rights would naturally follow. This was a very non-threatening idea both politically and socially, and it was very popular with a lot of whites in the late nineteenth century.

By the 1890's Washington was the most prominent African American in the country. A number of presidents looked to Washington to advise them in matters of race. But other African-American leaders and intellectuals disagreed with him. They felt Washington's message would not promote the

Booker T. Washington felt African Americans should try to improve themselves within the existing system.

advancement of the civil rights of African Americans. They did not feel that Washington had the right to speak for all African Americans, and they did not trust his reliance on wealthy white Northerners for assistance. W. E. B. Du Bois was one of those who did not care to be represented by Booker T. Washington.

Du Bois completely rejected Washington's willingness to avoid rocking the racial boat. He called on African Americans everywhere to fight for political power, civil rights, integration, and higher education for African-American youth. Du Bois even published an essay criticizing Washington's theories, "Of Mr. Booker T. Washington and Others," which appeared in a collection called *The Souls of Black Folk*.[2]

Mary Church Terrell was left in a difficult position. She agreed with Du Bois' vision of equality, but also appreciated the efforts of her friend, Washington, on behalf of his race. After her visit to the commencement ceremonies at the Tuskegee Institute, where Washington was the principal, Terrell had grown to appreciate Washington's efforts to train the masses of African Americans to earn a decent living. Students were taught carpentry, sewing and modern farming. Washington believed in education of the hands and heart. He felt that work and discipline were more important than political and social rights.

Terrell was aware that no race of people could succeed financially without a well-trained working class.

However, she also felt that Washington spent too much of his time and energy promoting the idea of training for a trade. He seemed to ignore other important ideas in the larger cause they had all been fighting for. She especially didn't appreciate that Washington tended to make college-educated African Americans, such as herself, appear foolish for believing that higher education could make a difference in the struggle for equality. Washington invited Terrell to Tuskegee's graduation, "After I had seen Tuskegee, I had a greater admiration for Washington."[3]

In 1905, Du Bois took an historic step. He was founder of the Niagara Movement, which was dedicated chiefly to attacking the accommodationist platforms of Booker T. Washington. The small organization, which met annually until 1909, was seriously weakened by internal disagreements. Washington's strong public opposition to the Niagara Movement damaged the organization even more.

In September of 1908, an article written by William English Walling, called "Race War in the North," was printed in the Springfield Independent newspaper.[4] The article described the cruelty being carried out against African Americans across the United States. It ended with a call for a powerful body of citizens to come to their aid stating:

> We call upon all believers in democracy to join in a National conference for the discussion of present evils,

The voicing of the protest, and the renewal of the
Struggle for civil and political liberty.[5]

Sixty prominent black and white people would
answer this call. Among them were W.E.B. DuBois and
Mary Church Terrell.

These citizens agreed to organize a national conference in New York City in order to examine the issue of
race. This meeting, which took place on February 12,
1909, marked the formation of the National Association
for the Advancement of Colored People (NAACP).

Terrell became one of the founding members,
as did another African-American woman, Ida B.
Wells-Barnett. Wells-Barnett was the journalist whose
moving articles focused national attention on the many
lynchings taking place in America, including that of
Terrell's friend Tom Moss years earlier.

Terrell responded to the "call" without hesitation.
"I traveled a thousand miles to attend the first meeting
of the NAACP in New York," she remembered.[6] She
interrupted her lectures in the South as soon as
the telegram urging her to come to New York for the
meeting reached her in New Orleans.

She was very much in favor of an organization
dedicated to achieving civil rights. She felt it was her
duty to help in any way she could. "When I joined the
NAACP, my husband was warned that my actions
would ruin his career."[7] The decision to take part in the
organization was difficult for many people. She noted,

"I was severely criticized because I joined the NAACP"[8] which African Americans hesitated or refused outright to support. Some were afraid that they would lose their jobs if they joined. Some thought they could become a target for revenge. It took a great deal of bravery to join the NAACP when it first began.

Others who came to the first meeting of the NAACP included suffragette leaders Josephine Ruffin, Inez Mulholland, and Mary Talbert. Others were Congressman George Henry White, pacifists Jane Addams and Fanny Garrison Villard, lawyer Clarence Darrow, educator John Dewey, and journalists Charles Edward Russell, Lincoln Steffens and Ray Stannard Baker were among the founders. Terrell made new friends and was invited to lunch with Jane Addams many times after meetings.[9]

After she served on the NAACP's executive committee, Terrell created a branch of the organization in Washington, D.C. She became its vice-president. It was important to have a strong organized force in the nation's capital. Washington, D.C., had changed tremendously since the days she had visited as a young woman. The city had been known at that time as "the colored man's paradise," but was now firmly segregated. Blacks could not attend the theater without sitting in the low-quality seats reserved for them. They could not visit certain hotels or restaurants. They could not purchase a home outside of slum areas of the city.

Much of the work of the NAACP was in fighting discrimination laws through legal action. The NAACP took on legal challenges that tested the laws of America's Constitution. These lawsuits made the NAACP a powerful force for change, even during its early years.

The Supreme Court believed that "separate but equal," was a reasonable solution to race questions. This was the basis for the Jim Crow laws. The NAACP took on the challenge against these laws. The NAACP set its goal to have the Fourteenth and Fifteenth Constitutional Amendments enforced. This would put an end to all forced segregation.

The NAACP's fight to crush Jim Crow laws became more fierce. Meanwhile, the Supreme Court began the long, slow course to equality by weakening its support for Jim Crow laws. In 1915, the legal case of *Guinn* v. *The United States* caused the Supreme Court to overturn the "grandfather clause," a voting law designed to prevent African Americans from voting. According to the grandfather clause, if your grandfather didn't vote in the presidential election of 1860 (before the abolition of slavery), you couldn't vote either. The grandchildren of former slaves, therefore, could not vote. The NAACP brought a challenge to the Supreme Court to end the grandfather clause.

The NAACP also began to work on the problem of segregation, which forced blacks to live and gather in different places than whites. In a 1917 legal case, the Supreme Court decided that a Louisville city rule forcing blacks to live in certain sections of the city was unlawful. This ruling set the example for other legal challenges of its kind.

The NAACP decided that one of its first major battles was to force the creation of anti-lynching laws. The issue was an emotional one for Terrell because her childhood friend, Tom Moss, had been lynched. A common practice of lynching had swept across America following the Civil War. Many African Americans did not feel safe voicing their opinions for fear of being killed by racists.

To focus national attention on the lynching problem, the NAACP published a complete review of lynching records in 1919. This review was titled *Thirty Years of Lynching in the United States, 1889-1918*. Seven NAACP leaders risked their own lives in order to find out about the firsthand details behind the murders of so many African Americans.

The efforts of Terrell and other NAACP members led to several anti-lynching laws that passed in the House of Representatives. Yet, once the laws reached the Senate, they were always defeated. The civil rights movement had a long way to go to achieve equality for African Americans, but many more African Americans

Early members of the NAACP posed in front of their headquarters in Washington, D.C.

might have died without the NAACP's efforts. The number of mob lynchings declined, as the public became more aware of the horror.

The NAACP, which still exists today, used the courts constantly until all of the Jim Crow laws were withdrawn. But the fight took many years. In 1953, the NAACP joined forces again with Terrell as she fought against the discrimination laws in Washington, D.C. Using political pressure, picket signs, marches, sit-ins, and other methods, the NAACP remained a driving force in the struggle for equality. Terrell's dedication to the organization and its legal battles lasted her entire lifetime, from the NAACP's first meeting in 1909 to her fateful challenge in the Washington, D.C., restaurant in 1950.

10

AN AUTHOR
OF NOTE

Terrell used her education as a powerful tool in her pursuit of equality. In particular, Terrell developed her writing skills in order to have a greater impact on her readers. She was dedicated to fighting for her cause in any way possible.

Terrell received many requests for articles throughout her career. Her writing appeared in both black and white publications. "The first time I saw my name in print, I stood speechless," she said.[1] She used her writing to convey her feelings on racial and gender equality. Right after her marriage in 1892, Terrell was invited by Mrs. Josephine St. Pierre Ruffin to write the

Washington news report for *New Era.*[2] Ruffin had founded and published the magazine *New Era* in Boston.

Terrell wrote so well that the editor of *The Colored American* newspaper, published in Washington, D.C., asked her to write a column titled "Women's World."

She was also asked by the editor of *The New York Age*, T. Thomas Fortune, to write pieces for his publication.[3] Fairly soon, Terrell had contributed numerous articles to many different publications, including *The A.M.E. Church Review*, in Philadelphia; *The Southern Workman*, published in Hampton, Virginia; *The Indianapolis Freeman*; *The Afro-American* of Baltimore; and *The Washington Tribune*, among others.

Terrell was especially supportive of black newspapers. She felt these papers filled a necessary purpose in the lives of blacks living with racial discrimination. African Americans depended on these publications, black-owned and operated by black publishers, for an honest account of their affairs. White newspapers of the time tended to report only on the crimes and poor behavior of black people.

Terrell and other African Americans looked to black papers for knowledge concerning the accomplishments and progress of their race. Yet, Terrell also understood the benefits of spreading her voice against inequality through major white newspapers with larger numbers of readers. She contributed a number of articles to newspapers such as *The Washington Evening Star* and *The Washington Post*.

Despite Terrell's stellar writing career, which included many published works in distinguished publications, she claimed to have an overwhelming sense of dread whenever she sat down to write. She was very careful about the words that represented her to the world. Usually, her first drafts consisted of many words crossed out, changed or underlined. After much labor, her finished writing was a moving piece of literature for her readers and listeners.

Terrell frequently wrote for *The Voice of the Negro*, published in Atlanta, Georgia.[4] One of her most memorable articles for *The Voice of the Negro* was entitled "Christmas in the White House," published in 1904.[5] When her editor first asked her to write the article, Terrell was unsure if an interesting article about the holiday could be written with Christmas still several months away. She feared there would not be enough Christmas spirit at the White House that early in the year.

To her delight, after she visited the White House, she found more than enough to write about. She took pleasure in reporting about the charity of the president and Mrs. Roosevelt in her article. One of the things she noted was that the Roosevelts always gave Christmas gifts to two African-American boys whose father was a White House steward.

Most readers liked this kind of writing, but Terrell found that her more serious pieces about the treatment of blacks were often rejected by editors. She soon realized that most white editors preferred an article on the racial discrimination if it was written with white people's views in mind. Many of Terrell's articles about lynching and discrimination were too extreme for most newspapers and magazines. The editors would receive her writing submissions and quickly dismiss her ideas. They felt her ideas on the race problem would create too much of a stir with their readership.

Terrell's article, "Being a Colored Woman in the United States," came into the hands of a reader for a first-class publishing house. The reader was so impressed with the passion and clarity of Terrell's writing, that he forwarded her article, without telling her, to the editor of a popular white magazine. The editor of the magazine rejected her article outright. It frustrated Terrell that her work could receive such praise, yet be considered too strong to be published.[6]

Terrell also found that being a woman was an obstacle in the publishing world. Editors often would not publish her opinions because she was a black woman. As she wrote in her autobiography in 1940, "Nobody wants to know a colored woman's opinion about her own status or that of her group."[7]

After many of her articles on race and equality were rejected by major American papers and magazines,

Many of Terrell's articles about lynching and discrimination were too extreme for most newspapers. Pictured here are members of the Ku Klux Klan, a group of whites who carried out attacks against African Americans.

Terrell became discouraged. She finally stopped submitting articles on racism altogether.

But her writing had opened some important doors. Her article on lynching, for example, led to a meeting with author Mrs. Van Rensselaer Cruger, who wrote a letter to Terrell congratulating her on her writing efforts.

Mary Church Terrell decided to try writing fiction, something she'd always wanted to do. Terrell had noticed, and disliked, the fact that printed fiction stories of her time always showed the black man as a murderer or clown. Her stories were based on the strength and perseverance of black people. Her very first effort was accepted by the prominent newspaper, *The Washington Post*. This story, "Venus and the Night Doctor," became her first and last fiction ever published.

As with her articles, her stories were labeled too controversial. Editors again rejected her work. But the desire to publish her stories never left her. Terrell longed for the day when the duties on behalf of her people would leave her enough time for creative writing. Terrell thought that perhaps she could have been a novelist, short story writer or essayist, if she had more time to focus on her writing. For a while, Terrell would go to the Library of Congress each morning. There, she could work quietly without interruptions. Along with her short stories, she planned to write a novel. She collected information to help her write a history of black women from their days of slavery to the present. "Nothing like this has ever been attempted," she wrote in her journal.[8] But Terrell always found it more important to write for the betterment of her people. She put this before her own creative needs.

Terrell continued to write articles highlighting the achievements of black musicians, scientists, and important people in history. She also found the time to write a history of her own life. Her autobiography,

A Colored Woman in a White World, was published in 1940. In the book's introduction, she summed up her desire to use her own life story as an example of how to succeed in the face of great odds:

> In relating the story of my life I shall simply tell the truth and nothing but the truth but not the whole truth, for that would be impossible. And even if I tried to tell the whole truth, few people would believe me. I am well aware that truth will be interpreted by some to mean bitterness. But I am not bitter. I have recorded what I am able to accomplish in spite of the obstacles which I have had to surmount. I have done this, not because I want to tell the world how smart I am, but because both a sense of justice and regard for the truth prompt me to show what a colored woman can achieve in spite of the difficulties by which race prejudice blocks her path, if she fits herself to do a certain thing, works with all her might and main to do it, and is given a chance.[9]

11

THE TIRELESS ORGANIZER

All her life Mary Church Terrell devoted herself to speaking out for those who had no voice. In 1906 she helped black soldiers in their fight for equality after she heard of three who had been discharged without a hearing in 1906. During a racially motivated disturbance in Brownsville, Texas, a white man was killed and several others wounded. A civil rights organization, the Constitution League, called on Terrell to meet with the Secretary of War for the United States, William H. Taft. She requested that action against the African-American soldiers stop unless there was a hearing. Taft relayed the request to President Theodore Roosevelt, and another hearing for the soldiers was demanded.

During World War I, she was appointed to a clerkship in the War Risk Insurance Bureau. She was the only African-American woman working on the files. She soon became involved in a protest about the treatment of black women. This protest was sparked when Terrell, who did not look African-American, was assigned to a room reserved for white clerks. When her supervisor discovered that she was black, Terrell received a letter charging her with numerous violations and declaring her suspended from duty.

In response, Terrell wrote a letter to the colonel who had suspended her. She thought that her record would prove that the charges against her were false. But her request was denied. Terrell left to take a position with the Census Bureau instead.

Already upset about the racist treatment she had received at the War Risk Insurance Bureau, Terrell watched as fair-skinned black clerks at the Census Bureau were ordered removed from the white section when their race was discovered. Some of the black women asked Terrell to help them. They asked her to meet with the supervisor, hoping he would withdraw his orders. But he did not, and Terrell resigned in protest.

Around the same time she became involved with the War Camp Community Service (WCCS), an organization that helped African-American servicemen. She

During World War I Terrell was a champion of African-American rights in the U.S. military. Pictured here are officers of the "Buffalos," 367th Infantry, 77th Division.

helped to provide basic services for women and girls living in cities, too.

The WCCS established recreation centers for African-American soldiers returning from the war in Europe. The organization felt that the recreation centers would help returning soldiers make a smooth transition back into society. The centers would also serve the needs of their families by offering instructional classes for their wives and daughters. The group needed Terrell's help to select the women who ran these centers. Terrell toured Southern cities to weigh the impact of the WCCS's programs on African-American women and girls. She was very upset to discover the attitude of the Southern community towards these poor women.

Leading male citizens in some of the Southern cities fought Terrell's efforts to uplift African-American women. They argued that it was a waste of time to help people who lagged so far behind. Terrell prepared a report of the racist statements. She also reported the lack of playgrounds and public parks for African-American children. She reported the lack of clubrooms and meeting places for returning African-American soldiers or sailors coming from the war.

Although she had known that the South was not progressive in the fight for civil rights, Terrell couldn't understand how violent the opposition was to helping poor African-American women. She finally realized that most of the Southern whites were not in favor of any kind of black empowerment.

She was frustrated by this attitude, and by the attitude of some African-American leaders who did not actively push for integration and academic education for their fellow African Americans.

In 1920, the Republican National Committee asked Terrell to supervise the work of African-American women in the East. Her duties included talking with women's groups about exercising their newly gained right to vote, particularly for the Republican Party!

Terrell continued to work for the Republican National Committee for some time. She took the opportunity to work for the first woman to run for the Senate. She campaigned in 1929 for Ruth Hannah McCormick, who ran unsuccessfully for United States Senator from Illinois. During the Herbert Hoover presidential campaign of 1932, she was appointed supervisor of work among the African-American women of the East for a second time. Terrell remained a Republican until 1952, when she decided to vote for Democratic presidential candidate Adlai Stevenson, who had focused more attention on civil rights.

Terrell's entire life was devoted to public service in all of its different forms. She worked tirelessly for the National Association of Colored Women, continuing its community-based service projects. "Lifting as We Climb" was their motto.[1] Equal pay and access to child care were the NACW's most pressing goals. The organization recounted their achievements during the annual conventions.

Terrell fared less well in her work for another women's organization. In 1949, Terrell filed a lawsuit against the Washington, D.C., branch of the American Association of University Women, (AAUW). The branch had refused to admit her because of her race. The national organization of the AAUW, however, voted to reaffirm its policy of admitting any university graduate regardless of race, color, or creed, by a fantastic majority of 2168 to 65. When Terrell was admitted to the national body of the AAUW, members of the local AAUW resigned in protest.

But Terrell soldiered on in the fight against injustice and discrimination. She joined the campaign to free Rosa Lee Ingram. Ingram was sentenced to death, along with her fourteen- and sixteen-year-old sons, for killing a white man. On February 3, 1948, Ingram was assaulted by her white landlord. When she and her sons fought back, their struggle led to the white man's death. The Ingrams were found guilty of murder and sentenced to die, even the fourteen-year-old. A group of African-American women formed a committee to fight the guilty verdict. They called themselves the Sojourners for Truth and Justice. Terrell joined this group of women. As a result of their work, Rosa Lee Ingram was freed in 1959.

Terrell also fought a bill called the Defense of Marriage Act. The bill would make it illegal for blacks and whites to marry each other. She firmly believed that marriage should be decided by the individual not the state. Terrell, along with five other black women, went to Capitol Hill in Washington D.C., to meet with Senator Arthur Capper of Kansas. Capper had created the bill. During the meeting, Terrell soon realized that the senator was not even aware that a clause outlawing

Terrell dedicated her life to fighting injustices such as segregation. The fight for desegregation in public places like restaurants often led to counterprotests from some whites.

interracial marriage had been added to his bill. The bill subsequently died at the end of the Congressional section. It was never introduced again.

Terrell also became one of the first women presidents of the Bethel Library and Historical Society, one of the oldest organizations established by African Americans. "For years I attended the weekly meetings, supporting this important forum," she reported.[2] At first, her leadership met with criticism, but the members soon concluded "she could preside with ease and grace, plan with foresight, and execute with vigor."[3]

Terrell's strong ideas about race and equality helped African Americans work toward equality between the end of the Civil War and the beginning of desegregation. She won many honors for her achievements in civil rights and women's rights nationwide and abroad. During the 1950's, when her famous encounter in Thompson's Restaurant came to public attention, Terrell also fought successfully to prevent segregation in hotels and movie theaters in Washington, D.C.

For her tireless dedication to her fellow human beings, she was given honorary doctorates from Howard University and from Oberlin and Wilberforce Colleges. A school in Washington, D.C., was named for her. Several African-American women's clubs are also named in her memory.

The Smithsonian Institution, which collects important cultural materials, acquired a full-length oil portrait of Terrell from her family. The portrait is periodically displayed in the National Portrait Gallery in Washington, D.C., along with written profiles of her activities in the feminist and civil rights movements.

Terrell, after a lifetime of fabulous and unselfish accomplishment, died on July 24, 1954. She was ninety years old. She lost her brief battle with illness at Anne Arundel General Hospital in Annapolis,

The Mary Church Terrell House in Washington, D.C., has been declared a National Historic Landmark.

Maryland, a short distance from her summer home in Highland Beach.

Her death occurred just two months after the landmark Supreme Court decision of *Brown* vs. *Board of Education*, which declared segregation of American schools to be unconstitutional. Terrell never lived to see black and white children attending school together, but she helped create a world where such progress was possible. The life of every American has been touched by the work of Mary Church Terrell in her fight against injustice.

The Mary Church Terrell House, located at 326 T Street, NW, Washington, D.C., has been declared a National Historic Landmark. When she and her husband purchased the home, it stimulated the racial integration of LeDroit Park. Her turn-of-the-century home, now owned by Howard University, is included in the LeDroit Park Historic District, and is listed in the D.C. Inventory and the National Register of Historic Places.

Terrell's philosophy of life can best be summed up by her own words:

> *I will not shrink from undertaking what*
> *seems wise and good*
> *Because I labor under the double handicap*
> *of race and sex, but,*
> *Striving to preserve a calm mind with*
> *a courageous and cheerful*
> *Spirit, barring bitterness from my heart, I will*
> *struggle all the more earnestly, to meet the goal.*[4]

CHRONOLOGY

1863—Mary Eliza Church is born in Memphis, Tennessee, on September 23, to Louisa and Robert Reed Church.

1868—Mary's parents divorce, she and her brother Thomas live with their mother.

1869—Mary is sent to the Antioch College Model School for children in Yellow Springs, Ohio.

1879—She graduates from the public high school in Oberlin, Ohio.

1884—She graduates from Oberlin College.

1885—Begins teaching at Wilberforce University.

1887—Teaches at High School for Colored Youth, Washington, D. C.

1888—Begins studying and traveling in France, Germany and Switzerland.

1892— Marries Robert Heberton Terrell, a teacher and lawyer.

1895—She becomes the first African-American woman appointed to the District of Columbia School Board.

1896—Helps to organize and becomes the first President of the National Association of Colored Women.

1898—Daughter Phyllis is born.

1902—Husband Robert Terrell becomes the first African American Judge for The District of Columbia.

1904—Gives a speech to the International Congress of Women in Berlin, Germany.

1905—Campaigns for the Women's Suffragette Movement to help women win the right to vote. Adopts her brother Thomas' daughter, also named Mary.

1909—Becomes one of the first members of the NAACP.

1915—Assists in the formation of the Delta Sigma Theta Sorority at Howard University and becomes an honorary member.

1925—Husband, Judge Robert H. Terrell dies.

1940—Publishes her autobiography, *A Colored Woman in a White World*.

1948—Is awarded her Doctorate degree from Oberlin College and Howard University making her Dr. Mary Church Terrell.

1950—Files a lawsuit against Thompson's Restaurant to end segregation, using the 1872 and 1873 "Lost Laws."

1951—Receives an award from the NAACP for her work to end segregation in Washington, D. C., hotels and restaurants.

1954—Mary Church Terrell dies at her summer home in Annapolis, Maryland.

Chapter Notes

Chapter 1. Lost Laws

1. "Ask discrimination, end in licensed public places," *The Washington Afro American*, October 3, 1953.

2. "Mrs. Terrell Hails Decision As Boost For Freedom," *The Washington Afro American*, June 9, 1953.

3. District of Columbia v. John R. Thompson Co., *Supreme Court of the United States Case No. 617*, April 30, May 1, 1953 Argued, June 8, 1953, decided.

4. Coordinating Committee, For the Enforcement of the D. C. Anti-Discrimination Laws, 1953—flyers and handouts, *Moorland-Spingarn Research Center*, Howard University, Washington D. C.

5. Robert Taylor, "Civil Rights Court Test Looms in D. C. on Public Service": *The Pittsburgh Courier*, February 4, 1950.

Chapter 2. A Child of Privilege

1. Mary Church Terrell, *Mary Church Terrell, A Colored Woman in A White World*, (New York: Arno Press, 1990), p. 13.

2. Robert McHenry, *Her Heritage: A Biographical Encyclopedia of Famous American Women*, December 20, 1995, p. 13.

3. Roberta Church and Ronald Walter, *Nineteenth Century Memphis Families of Color 1850–1900*, 1987, pp. 90–91.

4. Ibid.

5. Terrell, p. 14.

6. Ibid., p. 15.

7. Ibid., p. 16.

Chapter 3. Education Was Her Life

1. *Robert R. Church Family Papers*, Memphis State University, Mississippi Valley Collection, letters, School papers, 1885–1904, Folder 1.

2. Annette Church and Roberta Church, *The Robert R. Churches of Memphis*, 1974.

3. Mary Church Terrell, *A Colored Woman in a White World* (New York: Arno Press, 1940), pp. 44–45.

4. Micheline Malson, Elisabeth Mudimbe-Boyi, Jean F. O'Barr, and Mary Wyer, *Black Women in America* (Chicago: University of Chicago Press, 1990), p. 167.

5. *Mary Church Terrell Papers*, Manuscript Division, Library of Congress.

6. Dorothy Sterling, *Mary Church Terrell, Notable American Women, The Modern Period*, Vol. 4, (Cambridge: Harvard University Press, 1980), p. 154.

7. Terrell, p. 31.

Chapter 4. A Born Activist

1. Jessie Carney Smith, *Notable Black Women*, Volume 1, Detroit and London, Gale Research, pp. 1116–1117.

2. Cookie Lommel, *Robert Church*, (Los Angeles: Melrose Square Publishing, 1995), p. 144.

3. Dorothy Sterling, *Black Foremothers: Three Lives* (New York: The Feminist Press, 1988), pp. 128–129.

4. *Mary Church Terrell Papers*, 1851–1962, A. C. Bilbrew Collection Los Angeles County Library.

5. Mary Church Terrell, *A Colored Woman in a White World* (New York: Arno Press, 1940), pp. 56–57.

6. Ibid.

7. Ibid.

Chapter 5. The Turning Point

1. Dorothy Sterling, *Mary Church Terrell, Notable American Women: The Modern Period*. Volume 4. (Cambridge: Harvard University Press, 1980).

2. Ibid.

3. Roberta Church and Ronald Walter, *Nineteenth Century Memphis Families of Color 1850–1900*, 1987, p. 90.

4. *Robert R. Church Family Papers*, Special Collections, University of Memphis, Mississippi Valley Collection.

5. Dorothy Sterling, *Black Foremothers: Three Lives* (New York: The Feminist Press, 1988), p. 141.

6. *Mary Church Terrell Papers*, Moorland-Spingarn Research Center, Howard University.

Chapter 6. The Lecture Circuit

1. *Mary Church Terrell Papers*: Moorland-Spingarn Research Center Howard University speech "The Progress of Colored Women", February 18, 1898.

2. America's Story from America's Library, The Library of Congress, <http://www.americaslibrary.gov/jb/civil/jb_civil_terrell_3.html>.

3. Progress of a People, from *The Progress of Colored Women*, <http://memory.loc.gov/ammen/aap/aapwomen.html>.

4. Jessie Carney Smith, *Notable Black Women*, Volume 1, Detroit and London, Gale Research, pp. 1117–1118.

5. Ibid.

6. Ibid.

7. Ibid.

Chapter 7. Women's Rights

1. *Mary Church Terrell Papers*, Moorland-Spingarn Research Center, Howard University.

2. Ibid.

3. Ibid.

4. *Mary Church Terrell Papers*, Manuscript Division, Library of Congress, Washington, D. C.

5. Mary Church Terrell, *A Colored Woman In A White World* (New York: Arno Press, 1940), p. 316.

6. Kathleen Barry, *Susan B. Anthony: A Biography of a Singular Feminist*, (New York: University Press, 1988), p. 56.

7. Ibid.

8. Ibid.

9. Terrell, p. 317.

10. Ibid.

Chapter 8. Serving Education

1. Mary Church Terrell, *A Colored Woman in a White World* (New York: Arno Press, 1990), p. 127.

2. Ibid., p. 142.

3. Ibid.

4. Cookie Lommel, *Robert Church* (Los Angeles, Melrose Square Publishing, 1995), p. 144.

5. Jessie Carney Smith, *Notable Black American Women*, Vol. 1, Detroit and London, Gale Research, p. 1116.

6. Ibid.

7. *Mary Church Terrell Papers*, Moorland-Spingarn Research Center, Howard University.

8. *Robert R. Church Family Papers*, Special Collections, University of Memphis, Mississippi Valley Collection.

Chapter 9. The NAACP Calls

1. "We call upon believers in democracy to join in a National Conference" *Springfield Independent*, February 12, 1909.

2. Mary Church Terrell, *A Colored Woman in a White World*, p. 193.

3. Joe Nazel, *Ida B. Wells* (Los Angeles: Melrose Square Publishing, 1995), p. 167.

4. Ibid, p. 170.

5. Ibid, p. 171.

6. *Mary Church Terrell Papers*, Moorland-Spingarn Research Center, Howard University.

7. Ibid.

8. Marianne Ruth, *Frederick Douglass* (Los Angeles: Melrose Square Publishing, 1991), p. 122.

9. Quoted in *Church, Robert R. Family Papers*, Special Collections, University of Memphis, Mississippi Valley Collection.

Chapter 10. An Author of Note

1. "The National Association of Colored Women," *Voice of the Negro*, January, 1906.

2. Ibid., p. 195.

3. "The International Congress of Women," *Voice of the Negro*, December, 1904.

4. "The Duty of The National Association of Colored Women to the Race" *AME Church Review*, January 1900.

5. Terrell, Mary Church, "Christmas at the White House" *Voice of the Negro*, December, 1904.

6. Ibid.

7. *Mary Church Terrell Papers*, Library of Congress, Washington, D. C.

8. Ibid.

9. Ibid.

Chapter 11. The Tireless Organizer

1. "Mary Church Terrell", *Tennessee Biographical Dictionary*. (New York: Somerset Publishers, 1994), p. 679.

2. "Club Work of Colored Women" *Southern Workman*, August 8, 1901.

3. *Mary Church Terrell Papers*, Library of Congress, Washington D. C.

4. Mary Church Terrell, "What it means to be colored in the Capital of the United States," *Independent*, January 24, 1907.

FURTHER READING

Fradin, Dennis Brindell and Judith Bloom Fradin *Fight On!: Mary Church Terrell's Battle for Integration*. New York: Clarion Books, 2003.

George, Charles, *The Struggle for Black Equality*, Farmington Hills, Mich.: Gale Group, 2001.

Rennert, Richard S. Editor, *Profiles of Great Black Americans*. Broomall, PA: Chelsea House Publishers, 1994.

Swain, Gwenyth, *Civil Rights Pioneer: A Story about Mary Church Terrell*. Minneapolis, Minn.: Lerner Publishing Group, 1999.

INTERNET ADDRESSES

National Archives Biographies
<http://www.inforplease.com/ipa/A0878413.html>

Family Education Network—Mary Church Terrell
<http://www.teachervision.com/lesson-plans/lesson-5088.html>

Carnegie Library African-American Biographies
<http://www.brightmoments.com/blackhistory>

INDEX